Hunters in the Sky

beak

eyes

claws

Some birds are hunters.

A good hunter has sharp eyes, sharp claws and a strong beak.

Magpies have sharp eyes and a strong beak.

BIRD ATTACK!

Contents

Claire Llewellyn

Story illustrated by
Steve May

Heinemann

Find out about

- Birds that hunt and kill for food, like magpies, owls, gannets and eagles

Tricky words

- hunters
- sharp
- eyes
- claws
- strong
- beak
- mouse
- ground

Introduce these tricky words and help the reader when they come across them later!

Text starter

Some birds are hunters and kill other animals for food. These birds have sharp eyes so they can see an animal, like a mouse or a fish, from a long way away. They also have sharp claws and strong beaks.

They can see small birds in a nest.

Do you think magpies are good hunters?

Magpies steal baby birds from other birds' nests.

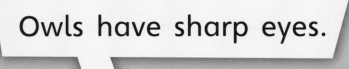

Owls have sharp eyes.

They can see a mouse on the ground.

Owls see well in the dark – they hunt at night!

Owls have sharp claws.

Do you think owls are good hunters?

Gannets have sharp eyes.

They can see fish
in the sea.

Gannets have strong beaks.

Do you think gannets are good hunters?

Gannets can dive at 60mph!

Eagles have sharp eyes, sharp claws **and** a strong beak.

Eagles are the best hunters.

Quiz

Text Detective

- What makes a bird a good hunter?
- Have you ever seen a hunting bird?

Word Detective

- **Phonic Focus:** Final letter sounds
  Page 10: Find a word that ends with the phoneme 'p'.
- Page 6: Find a word to rhyme with 'house'.
- Page 9: Find a sentence that is a question.

Super Speller

Read these words:

has   can   see

Now try to spell them!

HA! HA! HA!

Q What happened when the owl lost its voice?

A It didn't give a hoot!

In this story

 Jed

 Jed's mum

 The parrot

Introduce these tricky words and help the reader when they come across them later!

Tricky words

- note
- hello
- cage
- who's
- pretty
- head
- around
- robot cat

Story starter

Jed's mum is a vet. She looks after sick animals.
Sometimes she keeps an animal overnight at her home.
One day, mum had to go out. She left a note for Jed
asking him to talk to the parrot.

Jed
and the
Parrot

Jed looked at the note.

"Hello," said Jed.

"Hello," said the parrot.

Jed got the parrot out of the cage.

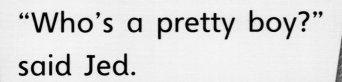

"Who's a pretty boy?" said Jed.

"Not you!" said the parrot.

The parrot sat on Jed's head.

"Ow!" said Jed.

The parrot flew around the room.

"Get back in the cage!" said Jed.

"No!" said the parrot.

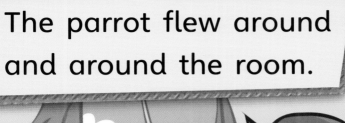

The parrot flew around and around the room.

How can Jed get the parrot back in the cage?

Jed got his robot cat.

"Mee-ow!" said the robot cat.

The parrot looked at the robot cat.

It flew back in the cage!

Mum got back and looked at the parrot.

"Shall we get the parrot out of the cage?" said Mum.

"No!" said Jed.

"No!" said the parrot.

Quiz

Text Detective

- How did Jed get the parrot back into its cage?
- Why didn't the parrot want to come out of its cage at the end?

Word Detective

- **Phonic Focus:** Final letter sounds
  Page 14: Find a word that ends with the phoneme 't'.
- Page 16: What words did the parrot say?
- Page 18: Find a word to rhyme with 'blew'.

Super Speller

Read these words:

back   not   get

Now try to spell them!

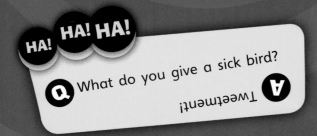

HA! HA! HA!

Q What do you give a sick bird?

A Tweetment!

24